Romans, Saxons & Vikings

Kings, Chiefs and Warriors

Martyn Whittock

Heinemann

First published in Great Britain by
Heinemann Library
Halley Court, Jordan Hill, Oxford OX2 8EJ

a division of Reed Educational and
Professional Publishing Ltd

OXFORD FLORENCE PRAGUE MADRID ATHENS
MELBOURNE AUCKLAND KUALA LUMPUR
SINGAPORE TOKYO IBADAN NAIROBI
KAMPALA JOHANNESBURG GABORONE
PORTSMOUTH NH CHICAGO
MEXICO CITY SAO PAULO

Designed by Ken Vail Graphic Design, Cambridge

Illustrations by Andrew Sharpe

Printed in the UK by Jarrold Book Printing Ltd,
Thetford

00 99 98 97 96

10 9 8 7 6 5 4 3 2 1

ISBN 0 431 05972 1

British Library Cataloguing in Publication Data

Whittock, Martyn J. (Martyn John)
Kings, chiefs & warriors
1. Great Britain – History – Anglo-Saxon
period,
449 – 1066 –
Juvenile literature
I. Title
942'.014

Acknowledgements

The Publishers would like to thank the following
for permission to reproduce photographs.

Lesley and Roy Adkins: p.17; Archaologisches
Landesmuseum Der Christian-Albrechts
Universitat: p.19; British Library: p.5, p.9, p.15;
British Museum: p.5, p. 7, p.11, p.25;
Kent County Record Office: p.23;
Salisbury & South Wiltshire Museum:
p.21; Sheffield City Museum: p.7;
Topham Picturepoint: p.29; University
of Cambridge, Committee for Aerial
Photography: p.27; R L Wilkins,
Institute of Archaeology, Oxford: p.4

The Publishers would also like to
thank Osprey Military for the
illustration on page 6.

Cover photograph reproduced with
permission of The British Museum.

Our thanks to Keith Stringer, of the
Department of History at Lancaster
University, for his comments in the
preparation of this book.

We should like to thank the
following schools for valuable
comments made regarding the
content and layout of this series:
Fitzmaurice Primary School,
Bradford-on-Avon, Wiltshire; Tyersal
First School, Bradford, Yorkshire.

Details of written sources

J. Campbell (ed), *The Anglo-Saxons*,
Phaidon 1982: 13B

G. Garmonsway, *The Anglo-Saxon
Chronicle*, Dent 1972: 1A; 5A; 7A; 8A; 9A

M. Harrison, G. Embleton, *The Anglo-
Saxon Thegn*, Osprey 1993: 3A; 3B

J. Morris, *Age of Arthur*, Phillimore
1977: 4B; 6A; 6C

A. Rivet, C. Smith, *Place Names of
Roman Britain*, Batsford 1979: 4A

L. Sherley-Price, *History of the English
Church and People*, Penguin 1968: 5B;
6B; 9B; 9C; 10A; 11A; 13A

**For Benjamin Jones, with love from
Uncle Martyn.**

Contents

Clues from the wars of the Anglo-Saxons 4

Anglo-Saxon weapons 6

How did the Anglo-Saxons fight? 8

Why did Anglo-Saxon warriors come to Britain? 10

The kingdoms of the Anglo-Saxons 12

Legends of the conquest – a man called 'Horse' 14

Legends of the conquest – Aelle and his sons 16

Legends of the conquest – Cerdic and the five ships 18

Wars in the west 20

The first Christian king 22

The king of Sutton Hoo? 24

Warriors in the north 26

The kings of the borderlands 28

Glossary 30

Timeline 31

Index 32

Clues from the wars of the Anglo-Saxons

Different kinds of clues have survived from the wars of the Anglo-Saxons. Some are shown here, but we have to be careful about how we use them.

The Anglo-Saxons ruled in England from about AD450 to 1066. In this time, different **kings** and **warriors** fought many battles. Until AD789 most of these battles were fought against other Anglo-Saxons or the **British** people. After this, many battles were fought against **Viking** invaders. This book is about the wars of the Anglo-Saxons before the coming of the Vikings.

Source B

AD530. In this year Cerdic and Cynric captured the Isle of Wight and killed a few men.

This is from a book called 'The Anglo-Saxon Chronicle'. It tells the story of the arrival of Anglo-Saxon warriors in southern Britain. This was written about 350 years after this battle, so can we really trust it?

A later Anglo-Saxon changed the words of this source. He changed it to 'killed many men'. He probably thought this sounded more exciting!

Source A

This is the handle and part of the blade of a sword. It comes from Finglesham, in Kent, and was made in about AD500. Things made from iron and steel rust. This can make it hard to understand what it really looked like.

Source C

This drawing of warriors was done in about AD1000. It seems to show us what Anglo-Saxon warriors looked like, but it was really copied from another book. The other book was made in about AD820. It was not made in England – it was made in France.

Source D

This helmet belonged to a rich warrior. He was probably a king who was buried in about AD625. It comes from Sutton Hoo, in Suffolk. In fact, very few warriors were rich enough to own helmets. Only two other Anglo-Saxon helmets have ever been found.

Anglo-Saxon weapons

Anglo-Saxon warriors used many different weapons. The kind of weapon a warrior used depended on how rich he was.

The most expensive weapons were swords, helmets and **chainmail** coats. Only the richest **kings** and their **warriors** could afford these. Shields were carried too. The first Anglo-Saxon shields were round and made from wood. In the middle was an iron plate called a 'boss'. Poorer warriors used spears and a knife, called a 'scramasax'. Sometimes axes were used.

Source A

On top of the helmets shone statues of boars, covered with gold. The fierce hearted boar guarded the warriors.

This is part of a poem called 'Beowulf', written in the eighth century.

A modern artist's idea of an Anglo-Saxon battle, fought in AD655.

Source B

This figure of a wild boar is from the top of an Anglo-Saxon helmet. The helmet comes from Benty Grange, in Derbyshire. It was made in the late seventh century.

Source C

Hold your shields right.
Show courage...
Never have sixty
swordsmen fought
more bravely.
A wounded warrior fell.
He said his ring-coat
was cut apart and his
helmet was smashed.

This is from a poem called 'The Fight at Finnsburg'. It describes a fifth-century battle but was written much later.

Source D

A shield found buried at Sutton Hoo, Suffolk. It was buried in about AD625. The 'boss' in the middle of the shield and the other metal decorations are from Anglo-Saxon times. The round wooden part of the shield is modern. This is because the original wooden part rotted away. The round part is covered with leather. This is modern too.

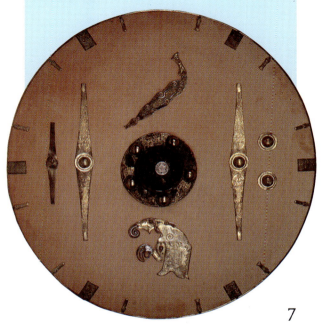

How do we know?

Sources A and B show that some rich warriors wore helmets with figures of wild boars on top. Sources C and D show that some warriors used shields. Source C also mentions swords, a helmet and a chainmail 'ring-coat'.

How did the Anglo-Saxons fight?

The first Anglo-Saxons fought on foot. Later, horses were used. Even then they were only used to carry warriors to battle.

Anglo-Saxon armies

Anglo-Saxon armies were often small. An army could be as few as 35 **warriors**. They were the bodyguards of a **lord**. Poorer men, called **ceorls**, carried food for the army. They also did the fighting that did not need much skill.

Most battles were hand-to-hand fights between warriors. The warriors would fight to the death to defend their lord. Some warriors had the job of defending their lord with shields. Some carried his sword for him.

Shield walls

At the start of a battle, warriors stood with their shields together. This was called the 'scildburh'. This means 'shieldfort'. They threw spears at the enemy and crashed into them. They tried to break through the lines of the enemy.

Source A

The battle cry should not be shouted until both lines have met. Only inexperienced men and cowards shout out from a distance. The enemy is more frightened if the shock of the battle cry happens when the weapons strike.

The Roman writer Vegetius describes battle cries used by German warriors, like the Anglo-Saxons. He wrote in AD400.

Source B

The warlike warriors turned back amidst the heaps of dead. They now had time to take from their hated enemies the shields and swords and the gleaming helmets. The precious treasures.

The poem 'Judith' describes warriors stripping weapons from the dead. It was written in about AD975.

Battle cries

Warriors shouted together as they fought. This frightened the enemy. Roman writers said they shouted as they crashed into their enemies. An Anglo-Saxon battle cry was 'Ut, Ut' ('Out, Out'). Christian warriors sometimes shouted 'Godemite' ('God Almighty'). These are recorded in accounts of battles.

Fighting for treasure

After a battle the winning warriors would take the weapons and treasure from those they had killed.

Source C

An eleventh-century picture. On the left is a **king**, protected by his shield-carrier. The battle is a hand-to-hand fight, on foot.

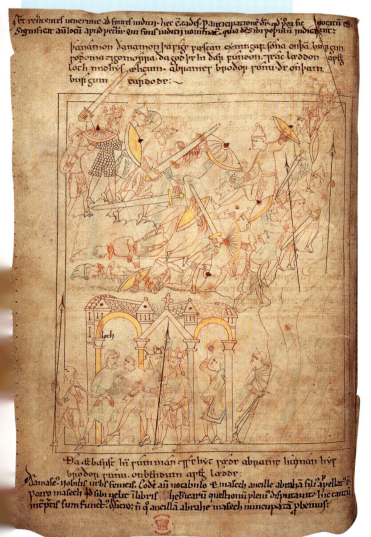

How do we know?

Source A shows that warriors used battle cries to frighten their enemies. Source B shows that warriors stripped weapons and treasure from dead enemies. Source C tells us that Anglo-Saxons fought on foot, and that kings were protected by shield carriers.

9

Why did Anglo-Saxon warriors come to Britain?

In AD410, the Romans could no longer defend Britain. They had trouble defending Rome itself from attacks. The Roman Emperor told the British to defend themselves. After this, people from northern Europe came to Britain. They took over land in eastern Britain. We call them the Anglo-Saxons.

Who were the Anglo-Saxons?

The newcomers were from German tribes called Angles, Saxons, Jutes, Frisians and Franks. They later called themselves the English. Romans called them 'Saxons' and **barbarians**. Later historians call them 'Anglo-Saxons'. The parts of Britain they took over became England.

Why did the Anglo-Saxons come?

The Romans had paid German **warriors** to fight for them. When the Romans stopped defending Britain, the **British** also paid German warriors to fight for them. They paid Anglo-Saxons to fight for them. Other Anglo-Saxons came for other reasons. Some wanted new land to settle on. Some came to raid and steal.

Source A

The British took up weapons. Risking their lives they freed their cities from the barbarians attacking them.

This was written by the historian Zosimus in about AD500. He lived far from Britain. He recorded stories he heard about Britain.

Source B

To defend themselves from northern barbarians, the British invited to Britain the vile, unspeakable Saxons. People hated by God and man.

A British writer named Gildas wrote this. It may have been written as early as AD480.

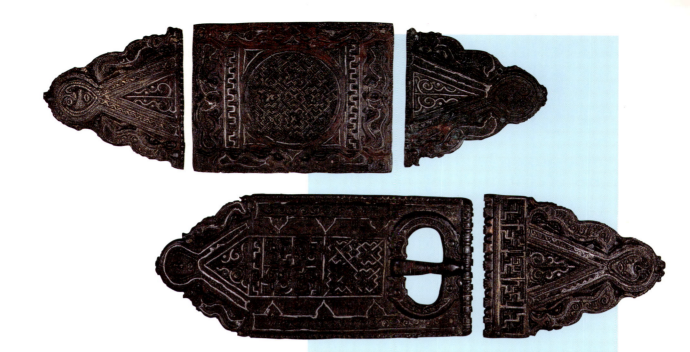

How do we know?

Source A shows that the British had to defend themselves from attacks when there were no more Roman soldiers to do it for them. Source B says that the British paid Anglo-Saxon warriors to defend Britain for them. These warriors might have worn buckles like the one in Source C.

But we must be careful. Zosimus never came to Britain. Gildas was **biased**. He hated the Saxons and only ever wrote bad things about them. We cannot be sure if we can trust what these people wrote.

Source C

This belt buckle is from an Anglo-Saxon grave at Mucking, in Essex. It is like those worn by Roman officials and soldiers.

Trouble at home

Some Anglo-Saxons came to Britain because they had problems at home. Their population was going up. There was not enough land for everyone. The sea was flooding villages. It was time to move.

Also, fierce tribes were threatening them. The rich land of Britain offered them a chance to find new homes.

11

The kingdoms of the Anglo-Saxons

Anglo-Saxon leaders took over parts of Britain. They ruled these areas as kings. There were many Anglo-Saxon kingdoms, and many Anglo-Saxon kings.

The first Anglo-Saxons **warriors** came to Britain for different reasons. Some came to raid. Some came to work for the **British**. These warriors came in groups. These groups were led by their chiefs, or **lords**. Soon these warriors and their lords took land and ruled it themselves.

Lords and warriors

Each lord had followers who were warriors. They fought for him and he gave them treasure. They were called 'gesiths' and later 'thegns'. The most powerful gesiths were called 'eorls' and later **'ealdormen'**.

The lords who captured a lot of land began to call themselves **kings**. By AD600 there were many such kings, each with his own kingdom. Some kingdoms were quite large, some were very small. These kings fought each other and the British.

Source A

Almost all the thirty royal commanders who had come to help Penda were killed. Among them was Ethelhere, king of the East Angles.

This was written by an Anglo-Saxon named Bede. It describes a battle fought in AD655. Bede tells how the Anglo-Saxon King Penda of Mercia was supported by 30 other kings. Bede wrote in about AD731.

Source B

Woden
Caesar
Tyttwian
Trygil
Hrothmund
Hryp
Wilhelm
Wehha
Wuffa

This is part of a list of East Anglian kings. This list was put together in about AD812, almost 300 years after the death of the last king on the list.

'Sons of the gods ... '

Anglo-Saxon kings often claimed their families had come from their gods. They usually claimed that their ancestor was the god Woden. One kingdom, the East Saxons, claimed their kings were descended from another god – Seaxnet.

Kings made these claims to show that they thought they were special people. In East Anglia the kings even claimed that they were descended from Caesar the Roman Emperor as well!

The main kingdoms by the early seventh century (AD600).

British Kingdoms
Anglo-Saxon Kingdoms

How do we know?

Source A shows there were many kings in Anglo-Saxon England. Penda was supported by 30 kings. Some were Anglo-Saxons. Others were British.

Source B shows that Anglo-Saxon kings claimed that gods had started their families. They usually claimed they were descended from the god Woden. The East Anglians added the name of the Roman Emperor to make them sound even more important.

Legends of the conquest – a man called 'Horse'

Anglo-Saxons told stories about how they came to Britain. These stories tell of the brave deeds of their first leaders. Some may be legends – stories which mix up facts and things which never happened. They are what people thought might have happened.

These **legends** tell how the kingdom of Kent started in about AD450. A **British** leader named Vortigern needed soldiers. He asked two Anglo-Saxon leaders to help him. They were brothers, called Hengest and Horsa. Their names mean 'Stallion' and 'Horse'. They came with three ships of **warriors** to Kent and were given the island of Thanet to live in. Vortigern married Hengest's daughter, Renwein.

The Anglo-Saxons revolt!

Hengest and Horsa said Vortigern was not paying them enough, so they revolted. They attacked the British and they destroyed cities. They killed many people and they stole treasure. They raided across Britain, then they returned to their homes in Kent. More warriors joined them from across the sea.

Source A

The brood of lion cubs burst from the lair of the **barbarian** lioness. They came in three 'keels'. This is what they call warships in their language. They first sunk their claws into the eastern part of the island.

This was written by a British writer named Gildas. It may have been written as early as AD480. The 'lion cubs' are Anglo-Saxons.

Source B

The first chieftains are said to be the brothers Hengest and Horsa. They were the sons of Wictgils. His father was Witta. His father was Wecta. He was son of Woden.

An Anglo-Saxon named Bede wrote this. He wrote it in about AD731.

Source C

There came three ships from Germany. In them were the brothers Horsa and Hengest. Vortigern welcomed them. He gave them the island that they call Thanet. In our language it is called Ruoihm.

This is from another British version of the story. It was probably written by a man called Nennius, in about AD800.

The end of Vortigern

The British people hated Vortigern. This was because he brought the Anglo-Saxons to Britain. He was forced to give up his throne, and wandered across Britain. At last he died. Some legends say he was swallowed by the earth. Some legends say he was burnt.

The oldest of these legends were told by British people. Then Anglo-Saxons told similar legends. They may have copied the older legends. As time went by, other people added things to the legend. They added things that were probably made up.

Source D

A picture showing Vortigern's death, dating from the fourteenth century.

How do we know?

Source A claims the first Anglo-Saxons came in three ships. They came to eastern Britain.

Source B tells us the names of their leaders. It says they thought their family came from the god Woden. This was probably to make them sound special. Source C was written later. The writer may have taken some of his information from Sources A and B.

Source D shows how some people thought Vortigern died. But it was made hundreds of years later. We cannot rely on it.

Legends of the conquest – Aelle and his sons

There are Anglo-Saxon legends that tell how the kingdom of Sussex began. They tell how it was started by a warrior lord and his three sons.

The Anglo-Saxon Chronicle tells this **legend**, but the Chronicle was not written until about 400 years later. We do not know how true the story is. Parts of it may be from very old stories and parts may just be made up.

Aelle and his three sons

The **warrior lord** was named Aelle. His three sons were called Cymen, Wlencing and Cissa. They landed in Sussex in three ships. They arrived in AD477.

Wars against the British

Aelle and his warriors beat the **British**. They drove the British back into the forests of Sussex. Aelle captured the parts of Sussex near the sea.

Aelle made an agreement with the British. This split Sussex between the Anglo-Saxons and the British.

Source A

AD485. In this year Aelle fought the British at the river Mearcraedesburna.

AD491. In this year Aelle and Cissa attacked Andredescester. They killed everyone living there.

*This is from The Anglo-Saxon Chronicle. It was written in about AD890. The river's name means 'the river at the **border**'. It probably refers to a border made after the battle. Andredescester was an old Roman fort at Pevensey, in Sussex.*

A battle at an old Roman fort

Later, in AD491, Aelle attacked a fort called Andredescester. This is at Pevensey, in Sussex. His warriors killed every British person inside the fort.

The Roman fort at Pevensey, Sussex. The Anglo-Saxons called it Andredescester.

How do we know?

Source A shows that later English people believed that Aelle divided Sussex with the British. The river's name probably shows there was a border between the Anglo-Saxons and the British. It also tells us that he attacked a fort and killed all the British there.

Source B shows that there was an old Roman fort that was called Andredescester, but this does not prove that Aelle fought there. The whole story may be made up, as it was written a long time afterwards – we cannot be sure.

Sussex place-names

The Anglo-Saxon Chronicle says Aelle first appeared at a place called Cymenesora. This is named after his son, Cymen. The place-name Chichester sounds like the name Cissa. The place-name Lancing sounds like Wlencing. It may be that the story of Aelle's sons was just made up to try to explain what the names of these places mean!

Legends of the conquest – Cerdic and the five ships

The Anglo-Saxon Chronicle tells the legend of how the kingdom of Wessex began. This kingdom was in the west of England. Its name means the West Saxons. It was started by an Anglo-Saxon who had a British name. The legend is very strange.

The **legend** says that in AD495 two Anglo-Saxon **lords** landed near modern Southampton. They arrived with five ships of **warriors**. One of the lords was named Cerdic. His son was named Cynric. The day they landed, they fought the **British**. The Anglo-Saxons won.

The beginning of Wessex

Cerdic and Cynric went on to fight many battles against the British. They captured the land around modern Southampton, and they took the Isle of Wight. They started the kingdom of Wessex.

Anglo-Saxons with British names!

Cerdic is not an Anglo-Saxon name. It is British. Other members of his family had Anglo-Saxon names! Maybe the legend is muddled, or it may show that some Anglo-Saxon and British people married each other.

Source A

AD495. In this year, two **ealdormen**, Cerdic and Cynric came to Britain. They came with five ships. They came to Cerdicesora. The same day they fought against the British.

AD501. In this year Port and his two sons came to the place called Portsmouth.

AD514. In this year the West Saxons Stuf and Wihtgar came to Britain with three ships. They came to Cerdicesora. They fought and beat the British.

From The Anglo-Saxon Chronicle, written in about AD890.

This boat, from Nydam, in Denmark, is from the fourth century. Cerdic may have used boats like this one.

How do we know?

Source A tells us a lot about legends of Wessex. It tells us the names of the first chiefs. But some of the names may be copied from place-names and not the names of real people at all. Perhaps these people never really existed.

It also tells us that the West Saxons are not mentioned until AD514. Then this arrival is like a copy of the arrival of Cerdic and Cynric.

Source B shows the type of boat which may have been used by warriors like these. It comes from a part of Europe where Anglo-Saxons lived before coming to Britain.

Sometimes they gave their children British names, sometimes Anglo-Saxon names. This would explain why some Anglo-Saxon royal families had members with both British and Anglo-Saxon names.

A very mixed-up legend

The legends about Wessex are very confusing. The Anglo-Saxon Chronicle tells us about two more arrivals of warriors, in AD501 and AD514. They sound like copies of the arrival of Cerdic and Cynric!

Cerdic and Cynric are never called 'West Saxons'. One story says that the West Saxons did not arrive until AD514. Then their leaders were called Stuf and Wihtgar. They were given the Isle of Wight by Cerdic. Wihtgar's name sounds like the name of this island.

19

Wars in the west

The Anglo-Saxons in the west of England were called the West Saxons. The kingdom they set up was called Wessex. Their story is told by The Anglo-Saxon Chronicle. This was written for the kings of Wessex in around AD890. But Wessex was a very complicated kingdom.

The first great **king** of Wessex was named Ceawlin. He was king after AD560. He won battles against the **British** and captured the old Roman cities of Gloucester, Cirencester and Bath. He took his armies into the Midlands but had to retreat. He was overthrown and killed.

Later people said he was a 'bretwalda'. This meant a great king who ruled many other kings.

Wessex grows larger

In the seventh century, kings of Wessex captured more land in the west. These West Saxon kings were named Cenwalh, Cadwalla and Ine. Somerset and Dorset became part of Wessex. The powerful Anglo-Saxon kingdom of Mercia stopped Wessex from capturing more land to the north.

Source A

AD626. King Edwin went into Wessex with his army. He killed five kings there and many of the people.

This is from The Anglo-Saxon Chronicle, written in around AD890. It describes an attack on Wessex by the Anglo-Saxon king of Northumbria.

Source B

From the Jutes are descended the people of Kent and the Isle of Wight. And those living in the province of the West Saxons opposite the Isle of Wight.

This was written by the Anglo-Saxon Bede, in about AD731.

Cadwalla captured the Isle of Wight. He slaughtered everyone there and replaced them with settlers from his own province.

This was written by the Anglo-Saxon Bede, in about AD731. Cadwalla was a king of Wessex. The people he killed were Jutes.

Source D

This bowl is from Wiltshire, in Wessex. It was made by a British craftworker, probably in Wessex. It is decorated in styles popular with British people.

Where was the heart of Wessex?

The Anglo-Saxon Chronicle says that the first Anglo-Saxons in Wessex arrived on the south coast, then they moved north. But **archaeologists** have found early Anglo-Saxon **settlements** around Oxford. These are all ignored by the writers of the Chronicle, and we do not know who they were. These people were later made a part of Wessex, but we do not know who their early leaders were.

Was Wessex really united?

The Chronicle says Wessex was a united kingdom, but people from the Jute tribe lived around Southampton and on the Isle of Wight. The West Saxons tried to kill them. There were also many British people who lived in Wessex. Sometimes Wessex was split up among many kings! It was a complicated kingdom.

How do we know?

Source A shows that Wessex was sometimes split among many kings.

Sources B, C and D show that not everyone in Wessex was a West Saxon. Some were Jutes. Others were British. The West Saxons wiped out some of the Jutes.

The first Christian king

One of the richest early Anglo-Saxon kingdoms was Kent. Its king was the first important Anglo-Saxon to become a Christian.

Kent was a rich kingdom. It **traded** with the powerful kingdom of the Franks. The Franks lived in modern France. They gave gold and jewels to the **king** of Kent, who used them to reward his **warriors**.

King Ethelbert of Kent

Ethelbert was a powerful king, who ruled from about AD560. He was a **bretwalda**. He was the most powerful king south of the river Humber. He married a daughter of the king of the Franks. She was a Christian but Ethelbert was not a Christian. He believed in Anglo-Saxon gods.

Christian visitors

The leader of the Christian Church in western Europe was the Pope. He lived in Rome. His name was Gregory. He sent a man called Augustine to Kent, to ask Ethelbert to become a Christian. Augustine and his friends arrived in Kent in AD597.

At first, Ethelbert was unsure but he let Augustine use an old church in Canterbury. This had been built in Roman times.

Source A

With the help of King Ethelbert, Augustine called the Christian leaders of the nearest British kingdom to a meeting. It was at the place which the English still call Augustine's Oak. It was on the **border** between the Hwiccas and the West Saxons. But they would not accept Augustine as their **archbishop**.

This was recorded by Bede, an Anglo-Saxon from Northumbria. He wrote in about AD731.

Source B

This is part of a book of laws, written for Ethelbert. It was written for him by leaders of the Christian Church. They could read and write. This copy is from the twelfth century.

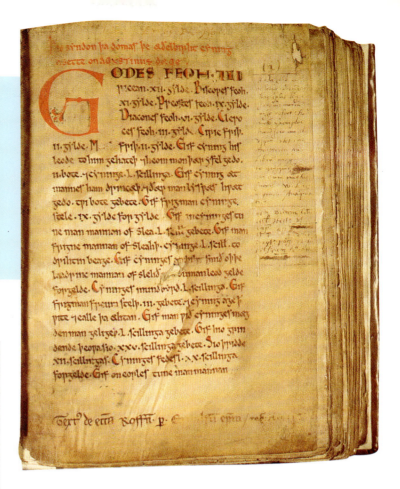

How do we know?

Source A shows how powerful a bretwalda Ethelbert was. He could make it safe for Augustine to travel far to the west. A king's power was not just seen in battles. It was also seen in how other people respected and obeyed him.

This source also reminds us that there were already Christian people in Britain. They were British Christians.

Source B shows how the Church helped Ethelbert. It had skills that he could use to run his kingdom better.

Ethelbert becomes a Christian

Finally Ethelbert became a Christian. He persuaded Anglo-Saxon kings in Essex and East Anglia to become Christians too. Ethelbert died in AD616.

In AD603, Augustine went to meet **British** Christians. The meeting was in the west of England. It was a long way from Kent but Ethelbert was so powerful that he made it safe for Augustine to travel this far. The British Christians refused to accept Augustine as their new archbishop. He returned to Kent.

The king of Sutton Hoo?

The richest Anglo-Saxon grave ever found was at Sutton Hoo. This is in East Anglia. The kings of East Anglia were powerful in the seventh century.

The East Angles were some of the earliest Anglo-Saxon settlers, but we do not know how they first came to Britain. Their royal family were called the 'Wuffingas'. They first became important in the seventh century.

Redwald king of East Anglia

The greatest **king** of East Anglia was Redwald. When he became king, Ethelbert of Kent was the most powerful ruler in southern England. Ethelbert had been king of Kent since about AD560. Redwald obeyed Ethelbert. He was baptized as a Christian. But when Ethelbert died, in AD616, Redwald went back to worshipping the Anglo-Saxon gods, such as Woden.

The most powerful king in north Britain in AD616 was Ethelfrith of Bernicia. He had driven away his rival, Edwin of Deira. Soon Ethelfrith became Redwald's enemy.

Edwin fled to Redwald, who protected him. Ethelfrith demanded Edwin be killed.

Source A

He raised a great army to make war on Ethelfrith. He allowed him no time to gather all his army together. He met him with a larger army and killed him. So Edwin not only escaped the plots of his enemies but became king.

Bede, a Northumbrian Anglo-Saxon, wrote this in about AD731. He was describing Redwald's attack on Ethelfrith.

This great gold buckle was found at Sutton Hoo in 1939. It belonged to a very rich person.

How do we know?

Source A tells us that Redwald caught Ethelfrith by surprise. He did not have time to gather all his army. This was why he lost. This helped Edwin to become king of Northumbria.

Source B shows that the person buried at Sutton Hoo must have been very rich and powerful. This may have been Redwald, as he was rich and powerful. But we cannot be sure if he was buried there.

Redwald becomes bretwalda

In AD616, Redwald surprised Ethelfrith and killed him instead. This made Redwald the most powerful ruler in Britain. Redwald helped Edwin to become king of all Northumbria.

The burial mounds of Sutton Hoo

In 1939 a very rich grave was discovered at Sutton Hoo, in Suffolk. A boat and priceless objects were buried under a mound. They were probably buried in about AD625. They must have belonged to someone powerful and rich. Redwald died around this time, so this treasure may have belonged to him. As a **bretwalda** he was both rich and powerful.

Warriors in the north

In the north of England were two Anglo-Saxon kingdoms – Bernicia and Deira. Together they made up the kingdom of Northumbria.

Ethelfrith unites Northumbria

The first great **king** of Northumbria was Ethelfrith. He was king in Bernicia. He drove out Edwin, the king of Deira, and he united Bernicia and Deira in one kingdom. He beat the king of the **Scots** at the battle of Degsastan in AD603. He beat the **British** at the battle of Chester.

In AD616, he was killed by Redwald, who was the Anglo-Saxon king of East Anglia. Redwald helped Edwin of Deira to become king of all Northumbria in AD616.

Edwin the bretwalda

Edwin later became a powerful king – a **bretwalda**. Other British and Anglo-Saxon kings had to obey him. Even people living on the island of Anglesey and the Isle of Man obeyed him. He built a great **hall** at a place called Yeavering, in modern Northumberland. Edwin became a Christian. He was killed in a battle at Hatfield Chase, in AD632.

Source A

He was like no other king before him. He made all of Britain obey him. Not only the English kingdoms but those ruled by the British too. He even controlled the islands of Anglesey and Man.

A Northumbrian, called Bede, wrote this, in about AD731. He was writing about Edwin.

This is how Yeavering, Northumberland, looks today. The marks on the ground show where a number of halls were built. The curved line was an animal pen. The squares show where the walls of the halls were.

Yeavering was the place where Edwin had his royal hall.

How do we know?

Source A shows how powerful Edwin was. He was feared by British and Anglo-Saxon kings. Source B shows there was an important **settlement** at Yeavering. The marks show large halls and other buildings there.

But we must be careful. Bede liked Edwin and wanted to make him sound great. And we cannot be sure which hall Edwin built at Yeavering.

Northern kings after Edwin

After Edwin died, two sons of Ethelfrith became kings. The first was Oswald. Like Edwin, he died in a battle fought against the Anglo-Saxons of Mercia and their British friends. The second king was Oswy. He was also a mighty king.

After these kings, Northumbria grew weaker. People disagreed about who should be king. South of Northumbria, a more powerful Anglo-Saxon kingdom was growing. This was the kingdom of Mercia.

The kings of the borderlands

In the centre of England was the Anglo-Saxon kingdom of Mercia. Its name means the kingdom of the 'borderlands'.

A **border** is where two different countries or peoples meet. The Mercians were on two borders. They lived next to the powerful Anglo-Saxon Northumbrians. They also lived next to **British** people living in Wales.

Penda of Mercia

The first famous **king** of Mercia was named Penda. He made friends with a British king named Cadwallon, who was a king in Wales. Together they killed Edwin, the king of Northumbria. This was in AD632. Together they destroyed parts of Northumbria.

Penda later killed King Oswald of Northumbria too. In AD645, Penda beat the king of Wessex, but in AD655, Penda was killed in battle by Oswy of Northumbria.

Mercia fights back

After Penda died, Mercia was harshly treated by Northumbria. But Mercia slowly recovered and grew strong again.

Source A

The treacherous king declared his plan to wipe out the entire nation. From the highest to the lowest in the land.

The Anglo-Saxon Bede describes Penda's hatred for Northumbria. This was written in about AD731.

Source B

King, not only of the Mercians but of all the people called the South English.

Ethelbald's title is written in a charter, AD736. A charter recorded a gift of land to someone, or to the church.

Source C

The earth wall of Offa's Dyke. This is in Shropshire.

How do we know?

Source A shows that Penda fought a terrible war against the people of Northumbria. But we must remember that Bede came from Northumbria and he did not like Penda.

Source B shows how powerful Mercian leaders became. They felt they were kings over many different people.

Source C shows the dyke that was probably built on Offa's orders. It took great power to have this built, but we cannot be sure why it was built.

Mercia in the eighth century

In AD716, a new king named Ethelbald came to rule Mercia. He was very powerful. He was obeyed by all the Anglo-Saxon kings south of the river Humber. In AD757, he was murdered by his own **warriors**.

The next king of Mercia was called Offa. By AD785 he was the most powerful king in all of England. He had a king of East Anglia beheaded. He called himself 'king of all the English people'. It was probably Offa who had a great earth wall built between Mercia and Wales, to keep British invaders out of Mercia. It is still called Offa's Dyke. Offa died in AD796. By this time, Anglo-Saxon England was under threat from new invaders from across the sea. They were the **Vikings**.

Glossary

archaeologists people who dig up and study things made in the past

archbishop an important leader in the Christian Church

barbarians people who lived outside the Roman Empire

biased taking sides, for or against a person

border where two different countries or groups of people meet

bretwalda a powerful king who was obeyed by other Anglo-Saxon kings

British the people living in Britain before the Anglo-Saxons arrived

ceorl an owner of a small amount of land

chainmail rings of metal fixed together to make a coat. It was used to protect warriors.

craftworker a skilled person who is able to make useful or expensive objects

ealdorman an important Anglo-Saxon leader

hall the large wooden house in which a lord lived with his family and followers. The most powerful lords had the grandest halls. The biggest halls belonged to kings.

king the ruler of a kingdom. Anglo-Saxon England was split up into a number of kingdoms. Eventually the kings of Wessex became rulers of all of England. Wessex was in the south and west of England.

legend a story which mixes up facts and things which never really happened

lords powerful Anglo-Saxon chiefs. Some lords went on to become kings.

Scots people living in modern south-west Scotland. They originally came from Ireland. Later they gave their name to Scotland.

settlement a group of houses, where people live together

trade buying and selling things

Vikings people from Denmark and Norway who attacked and settled in Anglo-Saxon England after AD789

warriors Anglo-Saxons who fought for their lord, or king. They were rewarded with gold and silver and lived with their lord. Some warriors went on to become important lords themselves.

Timeline – Romans, Anglo-Saxons and Vikings

AD1

AD100

AD200

AD300

AD400

AD500

AD600

AD700

AD800

AD900

AD1000

AD1100

Anglo-Saxon Age

AD400

AD410	Britain no longer part of the Roman Empire
AD450	Legends say Hengest and Horsa arrived in Kent
AD477	Legends say Aelle arrived in Sussex
AD495	Legends say Cerdic and Cynric arrived in Wessex

AD500

AD560	Ceawlin of Wessex becomes powerful
AD597	Christian preachers arrive in Kent King Ethelbert becomes a Christian

AD600

AD616	Redwald of East Anglia becomes powerful
AD625	Edwin of Northumbria becomes powerful

AD700

AD716	Ethelbald, king of Mercia, becomes powerful
AD731	Bede writing in Northumbria
AD785	Offa is the most powerful king in England
AD789	First Viking attacks

AD800

Index

Numbers in plain type (4) refer to the text.
Numbers in italic type (4) refer to a caption.

Aelle 16, 17
Andredescester
. . . . .16, 17, *17*
Anglo-Saxon Chronicle
   4, 16, 17, 18, 19, 20, 21
armies 8
arrival of the
Anglo-Saxons 10–11, 15
Augustine 22, 23

barbarians 10
battle cries 8, 9
battles 4, *6*, 7, 8, *9*
Bede   12, 14, 20, 21, 22,
       24, 26, 27, 28, 29
'Beowulf' 6
Bernicia, kingdom of 26
boats 14, 19, *19*
book of laws *23*
borders 16, 17, 28
bretwalda
. . . . .20, 22, 23, 25, 26
British 4, 10, 11, 12, 14,
       15, 16, 17, 18,20,
       21, 23, 26, 28
buckles *11, 25*

Cadwalla of Wessex
. . . . .20, 21
Cadwallon 28
Ceawlin of Wessex . .20
ceorls 8
Cerdic and Cynric
. . . . .4, 18, 19
charter 28
Christian Church
. . . . .22, 23, *23*, 24
crafts *21*
Deira, kingdom of . . .26

ealdormen 12, 18
East Anglia, kingdom of
. . . . .13, 24
Edwin of Northumbria
. . .20, 24, 25, 26, 27, 28
eorls 12
Ethelbald of Mercia
. . . . .28, 29
Ethelbert of Kent
. . . . .22, 23, *23*, 24
Ethelfrith of
Northumbria .24, 25, 26

'Fight at Finnsburg' . . .7
fighting methods . . .8–9
forts, Roman   16, 17, *17*
Franks 22

gesiths 12
Gildas 10, 11, 14
gods, Anglo-Saxon
. . . . .12, 13, 15, 24
graves 24, 25
Gregory, Pope 22

helmets 5, 6, 7, *7*
Hengest and Horsa 14, 15
horses 8

'Judith' 8
Jutes 10, 20, 21

Kent, kingdom of
. . . . .14, 22–3
kings and kingdoms
 . .6, *9*, 12–13, *13*, 16–29

legends . . .14, 15, 16–19
lords (chiefs) 8, 12

Mercia, kingdom of
. . . . .20, 27, 28–9

names, personal   18, 19
Northumbria,
kingdom of . . .26–7, 28

Offa of Mercia 29
Offa's Dyke 29, *29*
Oswald of Northumbria
. . . . .27, 28
Oswy of Northumbria
. . . . .27, 28

Penda of Mercia
. . . . .12, 13, 28, 29
Pevensey 16, 17, *17*
place-names 17, 19

Redwald of East Anglia
. . . . .24, 25, 26
Romans 10

'scildburh' (shield wall)
. 8
settlements . .21, 27, *27*
shields 6, 7, *7*
Sussex, kingdom of
. 16–17
Sutton Hoo
. . . .*5*, 7, 24, 25, *25*
swords 4, 6

thegns 12
treasure 8, 9, 12

Vikings 4, 29
Vortigern 14, 15, *15*

warriors
. . . .5, 6, 7, 8, 10, 11, 12
weapons 4, 6–7
Wessex, kingdom of
. . . . .18, 19, 20–1
West Saxons
. . . . .18, 19, 20–1
Woden . . .12, 13, 15, 24

Yeavering 26, 27, *27*

Zosimus 10, 11